PROTECTING OUR OCEANS

by Jeanette Leardi

Pictures To Think About

PROTECTING OUR OCEANS

Words To Think About

Read for More Clues

ecosystem, page 8
sewage, page 4
toxic, page 7

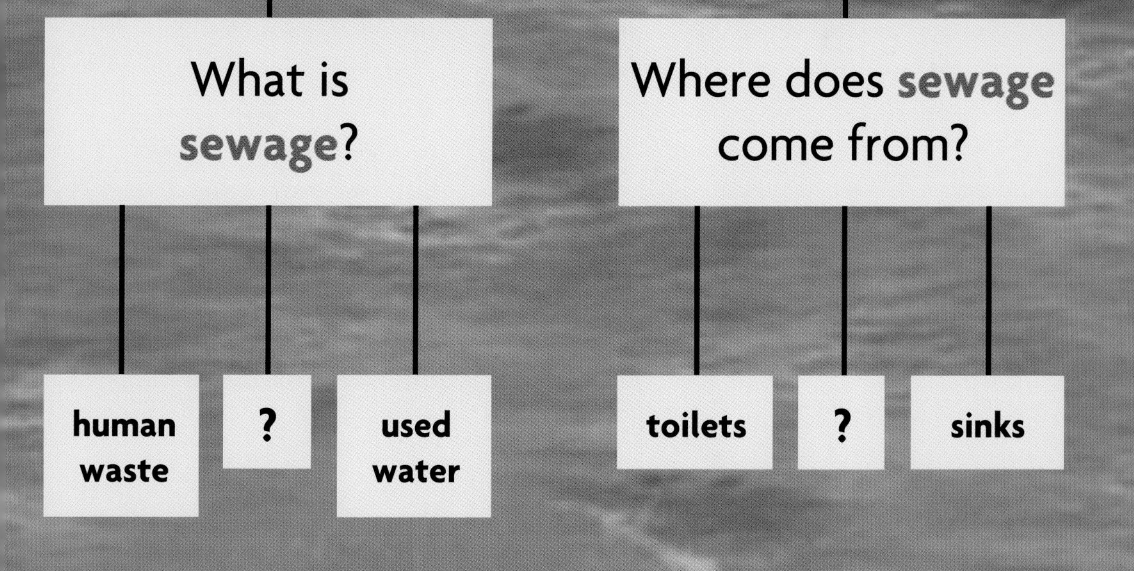

Introduction

A powerful storm rages at sea. A tanker ship carrying oil breaks apart. Oil pours out of the ship. The oil forms a thick blanket on the water.

Hours later, oil covers nearby plants and animals. The spill has **polluted** (puh-LOOT-ed), or dirtied, the water. The area will not be clean again for months or even years.

▲ This tanker's oil spill can harm ocean plants, animals, and seabirds.

Earth's oceans are all connected. Oceans cover about two-thirds of Earth. Oceans make up about ninety-seven percent of all water on Earth.

All living things need water. People, animals, and plants depend on water to live.

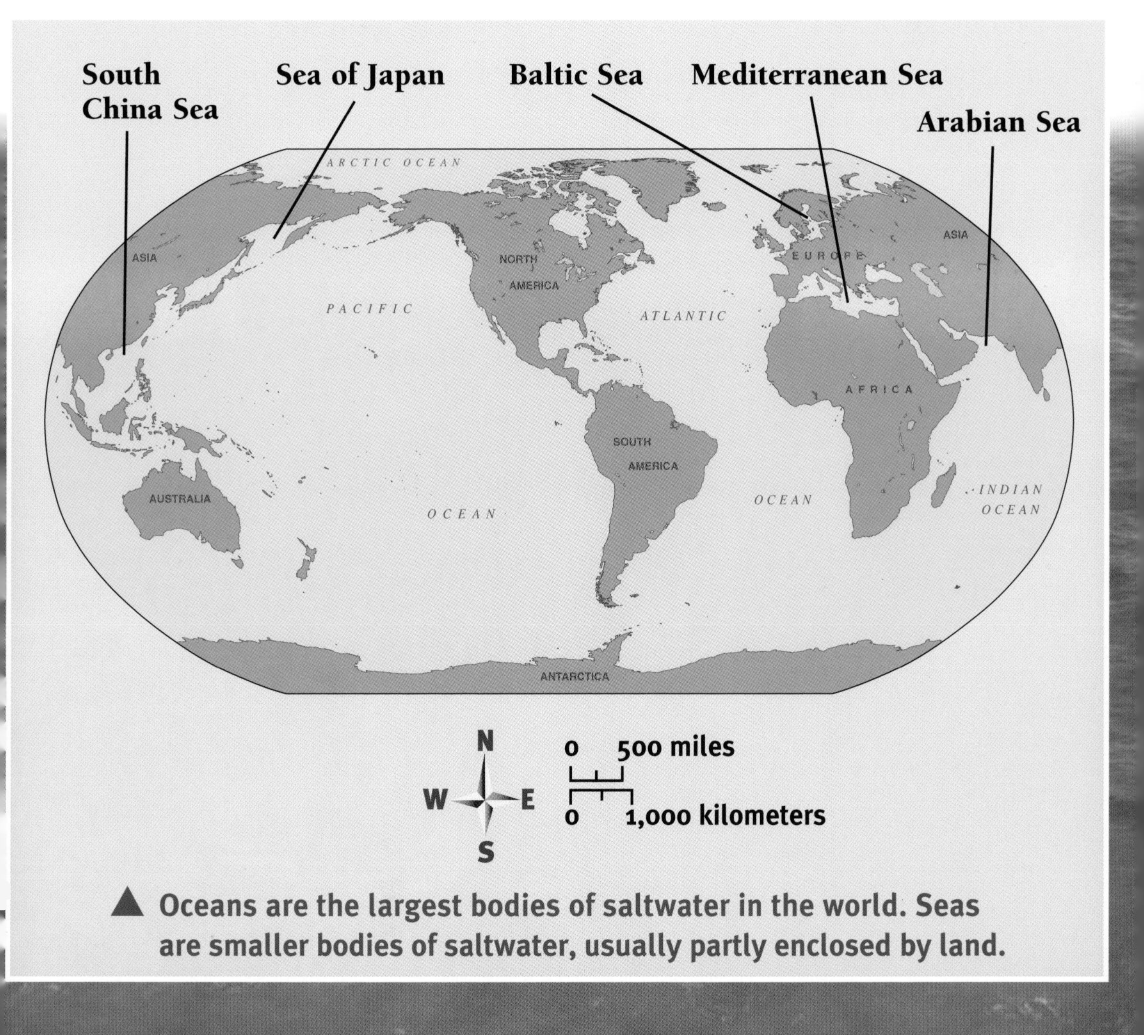

▲ Oceans are the largest bodies of saltwater in the world. Seas are smaller bodies of saltwater, usually partly enclosed by land.

How Does Pollution Happen?

It is a beautiful summer day. A family has come to the beach. The family wants to picnic and swim. They find the beach covered with trash. Plastic bags, cans, and broken glass bottles cover the beach.

The family sees **sewage** (SOO-ij), or human waste, in the water. It is not safe to picnic or swim. The whole area has been polluted. What causes pollution?

▲ People are one cause of pollution.

▲ People pollute beaches when they throw trash on the ground or toss it into the water.

Debris

Some people are careless about throwing out their trash. Most trash ends up in the ocean. Even the wind can blow trash into the ocean.

Another word for trash is **debris** (deh-BREE). Sometimes tires and used needles become debris. The ocean washes the debris onto beaches.

Not all debris ends up on beaches. Some debris floats on the water far from land. The debris can float there for years.

Some debris breaks down, or disappears, quickly. Other debris takes many years to break down.

1. Solve This

Use the information from the chart to answer the following:

a. **How many more weeks does it take for an apple core to break down than a cardboard box?**

b. **What is the difference in breakdown times between a foam cup and a plastic six-pack ring?**

Length of Time for Debris to Break Down

Debris	Length of Time
cardboard box	2 weeks
newspaper	6 weeks
apple core	2 months
foam cup	50 years
aluminum can	200 years
plastic six-pack ring	400 years
plastic bottle	450 years

Toxic Waste

Toxic (TAHK-sik) waste can cause sickness or death. Toxic waste can be hard to see or smell. Some **chemicals** (KEH-mih-kulz) are toxic waste. **Fertilizers** (FER-tih-ly-zerz) can also be toxic waste. People use fertilizers to feed plants and lawns.

Some toxic waste gets into the ground. Rain washes the waste deep into the earth. Water under the ground carries the waste to creeks and rivers. Then the waste goes into oceans.

IT'S A FACT

The Estuary

Fresh water from a river flows through a wide mouth or gateway called an estuary (ES-chuh-wair-ee). There, it mixes with saltwater from the ocean or sea. An estuary has plenty of food, so it attracts many different kinds of wildlife. Sea grass, salmon, shellfish, birds, crabs, oysters, and insects share this safe place.

Toxic waste can kill living things in an **ecosystem** (EE-koh-sis-tum). An ecosystem is all the things that live together and interact with their environment.

Sewage

Sewage is anything we flush down our toilets. Sewage is also anything we pour down drains and sewers. Sewage has **bacteria** (bak-TEER-ee-uh). Bacteria are tiny living things.

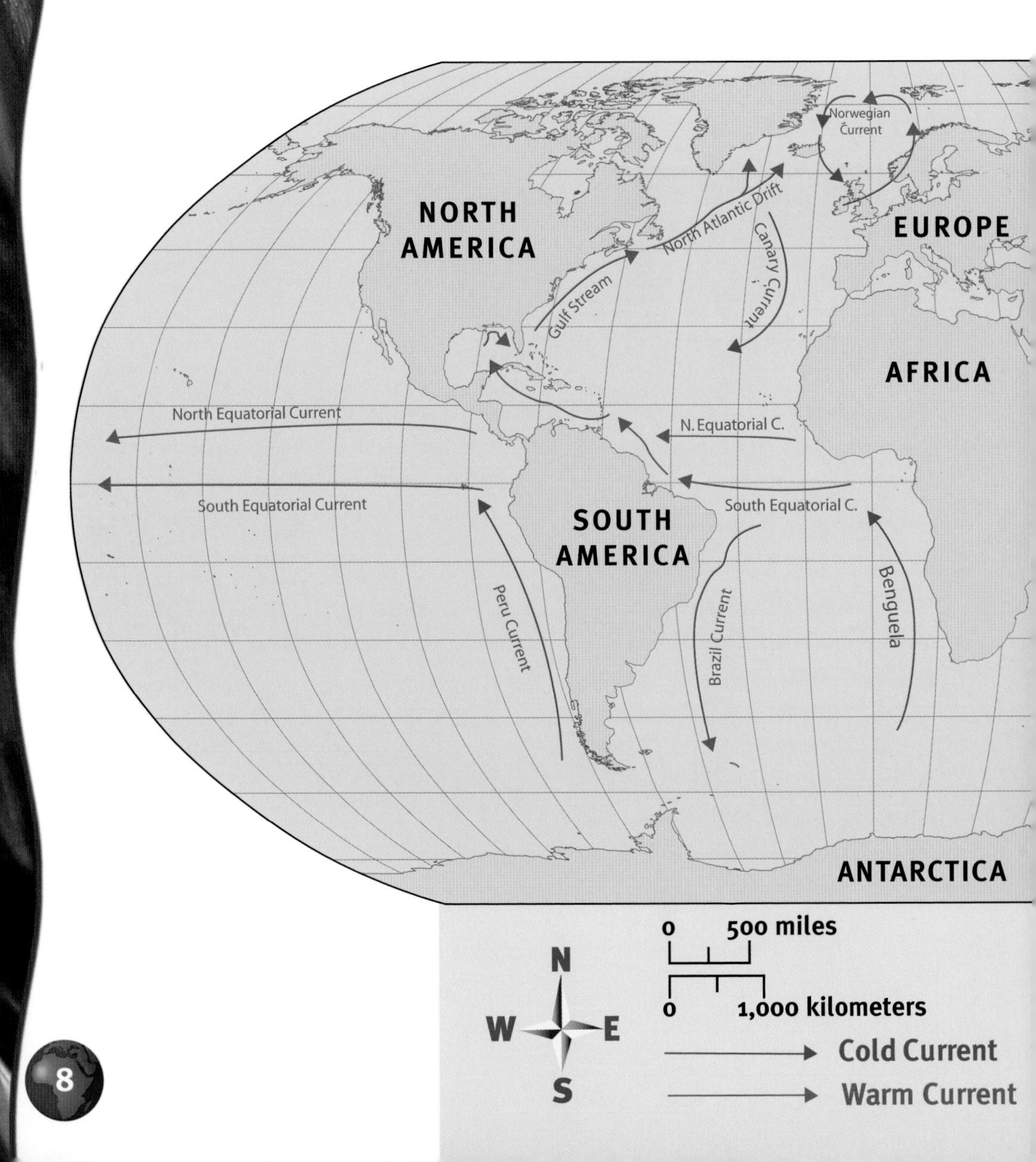

Most sewage goes to treatment centers. These places take out harmful bacteria. Not all sewage is treated. Bacteria in untreated sewage can harm and even kill living things.

Ocean **currents** (KER-ents) can carry sewage and debris very far. Sewage from the East Coast of America may end up on a beach in Scotland!

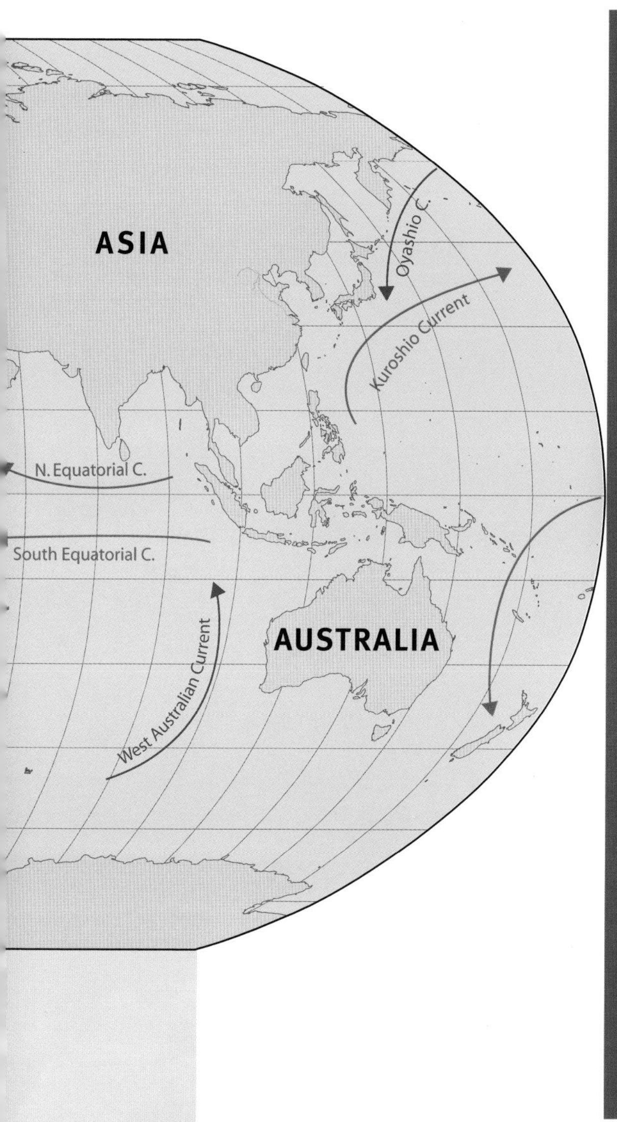

IT'S A FACT

Tankers spill oil into the ocean, and drill sites leak oil. But ten times more oil gets into the ocean because of what people pour into sewage pipes.

▲ Harmful bacteria must be removed from sewage before it reaches the ocean.

2. Solve This

International Coastal Cleanup 2003

Item	Number Found
bags	354,294
rope	131,197
plastic sheeting/tarps	89,234
balloons	66,532
fishing line	53,243
strapping bands	36,367
six-pack holders	36,236
fishing nets	29,967
crab/lobster/fish traps	27,928
medical needles	8,282
Total	833,280

The table shows the kinds of things found during a worldwide cleanup of beaches and oceans in 2003. About what percent of all dangerous debris is made up of bags?

Oil Spills and Leaks

Large oil spills hurt oceans and coastlines. Spills can happen when companies drill for oil in the ocean. Oil wells can blow up and spill oil.

Oil tankers can also cause spills. An oil tanker may hit rocks on the ocean floor. The rocks could make a hole in the ship. Then oil can flow out of the ship's tanks and into the ocean.

▲ There are sources of oil under the sea floor. People spend months at a time living and working on oil rigs in the ocean.

The *Exxon Valdez* Oil Spill

On March 24, 1989, the *Exxon Valdez* (val-DEEZ) hit Bligh (BLY) Reef, off the coast of Alaska. About 11 million gallons (37,000 metric tons) of oil spilled into the water. The Coast Guard, the United States, Environmental Protection Agency, and other groups used different ways to control the spread of thick, black ooze. Some of the oil was burned off. Floats were used to hold back some of the oil. Much of the oil was scraped off the surface of the water. But the Pacific Ocean's current spread the oil down the Alaskan coast. In fifty-six days, the oil had traveled 470 miles (756 kilometers). That's about the distance from Massachusetts to North Carolina!

▲ In 1989, the *Exxon Valdez* hit a reef off the coast of Alaska and spilled about 11 million gallons of oil.

EVERYDAY SCIENCE

Do oil and water mix? To find out, try this: Place some water in a saucer. Place some cooking oil in another saucer. Cut two small strips of paper. Dip one paper strip into the oil and the other strip into the water. Place the wet strips on some paper towels. Drop a drop of food coloring on each. What happens? Why?

From Land and Air: Acid Rain

Acid rain (A-sid RANE) is also harmful. Cars, trucks, power plants, and factories burn fuel. Burning fuel gives off gases. These gases join with water in the air. Strong acids form. The acids fall as mist, rain, sleet, or snow.

Acid rain harms plants and animals. Acid rain also harms soil. It can even destroy stone and metal. It can do a lot of damage to an ecosystem.

▼ Acid rain that falls on lakes and rivers sooner or later arrives at the ocean.

▲ ancient Sphinx affected by acid rain

POINT

Talk It Over

Discuss different ways oceans become polluted.

CHAPTER 2

How Does Pollution Affect Marine Life?

The ocean has many **species** (SPEE-sheez), or types, of living things. Each species is an important part of the ecosystem.

All living things in an ecosystem rely on each other. Pollution may harm one species. That species may be food for another species. Then the second species may go hungry. It may die, too. The ecosystem will change.

▼ This sea dragon looks like seaweed. Fish that might eat it pass by this plant look-alike.

Ocean Food Chains

Every living thing needs energy in order to live. Energy moves to all living things by a process called a **food chain**.

Many tiny living things are at the bottom of a food chain. With help from the sun, they make their own food for energy. But many living things cannot make their own food. They must eat other living things to get energy.

There are many different food chains in and by the ocean. Food chains are often connected. In the ocean, they often start with tiny living things called **plankton** (PLANK-tun).

◀ In some places, plankton are so thick that they color the water. Plankton can also affect climate. They use a lot of carbon dioxide (KAR-bun dy-AHK-side), one of the gases that may produce global warming.

◀ At the bottom of a food chain, the number of living things is far greater than the number of organisms at the top. So there's lots of food to go around.

Pollution and Fish

An oil spill can keep fish from breathing. The oil can poison the plants that fish eat.

Acid rain can keep fish eggs from hatching. Fish that eat debris can die. Toxic waste and sewage can blind fish. The waste can burn their skin.

Chemicals can hurt fish in another way. Tiny plants called algae (AL-jee) live in the ocean. Algae take in chemicals. Some chemicals make the algae grow too fast. Then the algae use up the oxygen (AHK-sih-jen) in the water. The fish do not have enough oxygen to breathe. This creates dead zones. Dead zones are places where algae have used up most of the oxygen.

Would it matter if these ocean organisms died off? Yes! Each organism is an important part of an ecosystem.

Giant Kelp: can grow over 12 inches (30 cm) a day. Kelp beds can be homes for other animals. Kelp is used in ice cream and other products.

Sea Urchins: live on seaweed and sea animals close to the top of the ocean. If they die, the seaweed will take over and choke out other sea life.

Peacock Worms: measure about 10 inches (25 cm). Tiny hairs help them feed and breathe.

▲ Dead zones can form anywhere on Earth.

Careers in Science

▲ These marine biologists are checking a reef to see if it is a healthy place for the plants and fish that live there.

Marine biologists (muh-REEN by-AH-lul-jists) explore ocean habitats. They study plants and animals that live in the ocean. They look for ways to keep the ecosystems healthy. Some marine biologists look for sources of new medicines and natural products.

To become a marine biologist, you must have a college degree in one of the sciences, such as biology, chemistry, or animal science. You will need further on-the-spot training in places such as ocean labs. If you want to swim among sea life, you must be very healthy, and be trained in deep-sea diving.

Pollution and Seabirds

Oil spills harm seabirds. The oil coats their feathers. The birds cannot fly. The birds may even drown.

Birds can also die from eating trash. Some birds get their heads caught in plastic rings. Then the birds cannot get free.

This bird struggles to survive an oil spill in Spain.

THEY MADE A DIFFERENCE

Ellen Browning Scripps

In 1903, wealthy Ellen Browning Scripps founded the Scripps Institution of Oceanography (oh-shuh-NAH-gruh-fee) in San Diego. She wanted everyone to have a place where they could learn about the oceans.

Today, people at Scripps conduct ocean research around the world. Hundreds of scientists explore such topics as how waves and currents work, and how ocean tides erode coastlines. Today, Ellen Browning Scripps' gift also helps train young scientists.

Pollution and Ocean Animals

Toxic waste hurts animals that live in the ocean. Currents carry toxic waste far distances.

Animals that live in the ocean may swallow floating debris. The debris can kill these animals.

Oil spills can harm many animals. Sea otters get cold if their fur is coated with oil. Sea otters can get sick if they are too cold. The otters can also get sick if they lick oil from their fur.

▼ This otter is not able to clean away the oil that coats its fur.

How Deep Is Really Deep?

Parts of the ocean floor are more than 8 miles (about 13 kilometers) deep. People began to explore the deep ocean only about fifty years ago. Freezing temperatures and high water pressure kept people away.

Today, technology (tek-NAH-luh-jee) helps us explore the deep ocean. Scientists use submersibles (sub-MER-sih-bulz). These are very small submarines. Some submersibles carry people. Others carry machines and robots.

▲ *Alvin*

Jason Jr. ▲

The ocean is important to us in many ways. We still have much to learn.

Look at the chart below. The chart shows some problems facing our oceans.

One Ocean, Four Names

Ocean	Percent Of Earth's Water	Deepest Known Point	Greatest Problems
Pacific Ocean	46%	-35,827 ft (-10,920 m)	Almost half of the world's shipping routes cross the Pacific. Oil pollution is a huge threat to ocean animals including dugongs (DOO-gaungz), sea lions, seals, turtles, and whales.
Atlantic Ocean	24%	-28,232 ft (-8,605 m)	Pollution from toxic waste, sewage, oil, and debris is a problem. Too much fishing has damaged ecosystems, especially on the ocean floor.
Indian Ocean	20%	-23,376 ft (-7,125 m)	Pollution from oil tankers is a huge threat to ocean animals including dugongs, turtles, and whales.
Arctic Ocean	3%	-18,399 ft (-5,608 m)	Ecosystems are easily harmed or destroyed and slow to recover. Whales, walruses, and fur seals are endangered.

THEY MADE A DIFFERENCE

Jacques Cousteau (ZHAHK koo-STOH) was a sea explorer. He invented the aqualung (AH-kwuh-lung). It allowed people to dive and breathe deeper underwater. In 1955, Cousteau went on a long sea journey on his ship *Calypso*. He photographed life in the sea. That and many other adventures were made into films.

Captain Cousteau drew attention to ocean pollution. He told the world that waters and coastlines must be kept clean. He showed how too much fishing would upset ocean ecosystems. He truly was a great modern scientist and teacher.

◀ Jacques Cousteau prepares to explore the undersea world in a shark-proof cage.

What's Being Done to Stop Ocean Pollution?

Some communities have cleanups. People meet at rivers, lakes, and beaches. The people wear rubber gloves. They carry large trash bags. They pick up debris. They want to stop ocean pollution.

Pollution affects the world. Many countries have rules to protect Earth. In 1972, the United Nations set up a special program. The program helps countries make their air and water cleaner.

▲ In many places, people work together to clean up their beaches.

▲ A worker cleans a rock on the beach of Green Island, Alaska, USA, after the *Exxon Valdez* oil spill in 1989.

International Coastal Cleanup

One of the best examples of cooperation to keep our oceans clean is the International Coastal Cleanup. Begun in 1986, it happens for one day every year. Volunteers from all over the world take part.

In 2003, 450,000 people from ninety-one countries picked up debris along waterways and beaches, and cleaned up reefs. Nearly 10,000 divers removed trash from underwater places. How much trash did they find? They found 7,550,000 pounds (3,424,622 kilograms) on land and 185,000 pounds (83,915 kilograms) under the water!

▲ Keeping oceans and beaches clean is everyone's responsibility.

Top Ten Types of Debris Littering the Oceans, 2003

Rank	Debris Items	Total Number
1	cigarettes and cigarette filters	1,922,830
2	food wrappers and containers	632,161
3	caps/lids	539,832
4	plastic beverage bottles	438,763
5	bags	354,294
6	glass beverage bottles	328,239
7	cups, plates, forks, knives, and spoons	317,447
8	beverage cans	314,738
9	straws and stirrers	273,105
10	tobacco packaging and wrappers	132,402
Total Number		5,253,811

3. Solve This

Look at the chart. How would the total number of debris items differ if all beverage bottles and cans were no longer littered?

Conclusion

All life in the ocean is connected. The living things depend on one another and on the environment. Hurting one often means others are hurt.

Ocean currents carry pollution across long distances. Debris, toxic waste, sewage, acid rain, and oil spills can hurt ocean life everywhere.

Countries need to work together to keep the oceans clean. We all need to protect the oceans.

▲ some ocean treasures

Use this chart to help summarize what you have read.

Type of Pollution	Main Sources	Effects on Ocean Life
toxic waste	house-cleaning powders and liquids	burns the skin of fish; blinds fish; harms the ability of fish to reproduce
sewage	toilet waste, bathtub dirt; sink and dishwasher food scraps	burns the skin of fish; blinds fish; causes sickness when swallowed
debris	paper/glass/plastic/aluminum litter; medical needles; car/truck tires and spare parts; trash spilled or thrown from boats; old fishing nets	chokes fish and birds if swallowed; strangles fish and birds
oil spills	oil wells; tankers	cuts off the supply of oxygen; causes birds to drown or keeps them from flying; causes sickness when swallowed; makes furry animals too cold
acid rain	factory chemicals; burned fuel	keeps fish eggs from hatching; kills tiny plants and animals in a food chain

POINT

Read More About It

You can read more about protecting the ocean at your school media center or local library. An adult can help you search the Internet for information.

▲ Everyone can work together to keep Earth's beaches and oceans clean.

Here are some ways people can help the oceans.

- Keep neighborhoods, streets, and beaches clean.
- Throw away trash safely.
- Do not waste paper, aluminum, or glass. Reuse or recycle them.
- Volunteer for a cleanup day.

We can help protect Earth by taking care of our oceans.

Glossary

acid rain	(A-sid RANE) a pollutant that forms when harmful chemicals in the air combine with water in the air to form acids, which fall as rain, sleet, or snow (page 13)
bacteria	(bak-TEER-ee-uh) tiny organisms that live in sewage (page 8)
chemical	(KEH-mih-kul) a substance that reacts with another substance to form something new (page 7)
current	(KER-ent) water that flows through the ocean in one direction (page 9)
debris	(deh-BREE) any piece of trash (page 5)
ecosystem	(EE-koh-sis-tem) living things, their environment, and their effect on each other (page 8)
fertilizer	(FER-tih-ly-zer) food for plants and lawns (page 7)
food chain	(FOOD CHANE) the order in which food energy moves from one living thing to another in an ecosystem (page 15)
plankton	(PLANK- tun) ocean animals and plants so tiny that you can't see them without a microscope (page 15)
pollute	(puh-LOOT) to make something harmfully dirty that once was clean (page 2)
sewage	(SOO-ij) human waste and used water that is carried off in drains under the ground (page 4)
species	(SPEE-sheez) the smallest classification of living things that have the same traits (page 14)
toxic	(TAHK-sik) anything that can cause sickness or death when a living thing takes it in (page 7)

Index

1. **page 6**
   a. 6 weeks;
   b. 350 years
2. **page 10** about 43%
3. **page 27** It would differ by 1,081,740.